QUEENS GATE SCHOOL
133 QUEENS GATE
LONDON SW7 5LE
TEL 071-589 3587

ESSENTIAL SPORTS

QUEENS GATE SCHOOL
133 QUEENS GATE
LONDON SW7 5LE
TEL 071-589 3587

ESSENTIAL SPORTS – NETBALL
was produced by

David West ⚇ **Children's Books**
7 Princeton Court
55 Felsham Road
London SW15 1AZ

Designer: Gary Jeffrey
Editor: James Pickering
Picture Research: Carlotta Cooper

First published in Great Britain by Heinemann
Library, Halley Court, Jordan Hill, Oxford
OX2 8EJ, part of Harcourt Education.
Heinemann is a registered trademark
of Harcourt Education Ltd.

07 06 05 04 03
10 9 8 7 6 5 4 3 2 1

ISBN 0 431 17373 7 (HB)
ISBN 0 431 17380 X (PB)

British Library Cataloguing in Publication Data

Smith, Andy
Netball. - (Essential Sports)
1. Netball - Juvenile literature
I. Title
796.3'24

PHOTO CREDITS :
Abbreviations: t-top, m-middle, b-bottom, r-right,
l-left, c-centre.

Front cover - Getty Images. Pages 3, 14b, 22l, 29bl
(Scott Barbour), 10l (Paul Cole), 11r, 15b, 24t
(Darren McNamara), 13r, 29t (Stuart Hannagan),
17 both, 28-29, 29br (Robert Cianflone), 10r, 19m,
30t (Tony Lewis), 19b, 20b (Daniel Berehulak), 26-
27 (Jeff Gross), 5t, 8, 26 both - Getty Images. 4,
7b, 11l, 12tl & tr, 16r, 25r, 28t (SWPix), 5b, 9,
12b, 13l, 14t, 15t, 16l, 18, 19l & tr, 20t, 21 all,
22r, 22-23, 24b, 25l, 27bl, & br, 28b, 30b - All
England Netball Association Limited. 6 both, 7tl &
tr - The Culture Archive.

Printed and bound in Italy

*An explanation of difficult words can be
found in the glossary on page 31.*

ESSENTIAL SPORTS
netball

Andy Smith

Contents

Athleticism, skill and fitness levels have improved as the game has spread out of the playground.

The Australian defence poses a problem for New Zealand's Julie Seymour, during the October 2001 Test match in Christchurch.

Introduction

The game of netball, a derivative of basketball, has been played for the best part of a century. At the top level it is an exciting, fast-moving, skilful sport, with players having to make instant decisions. Athleticism and fitness are essential requirements for this 'throw and catch' game, played for the most part by women. Although the rules allow for males to play, the games do have to be single sex. In the early days, netball was played almost exclusively at school level. By 1963, the first World Tournament was held in England, with eleven countries competing. In 2002, the International Federation of Netball Associations comprised 39 countries.

The playing uniform must have initials indicating playing positions, in this case Wing Defence.

History of the game

Netball began in 1895 when Dr Toles, an American lecturer at Madame Osterberg's Physical Training College in London, taught his pupils how to play a form of basketball.

BASKETBALL ORIGINS

Basketball had been invented in the USA in 1891. When Dr Toles brought his version of the game to London four years later, there were still no set rules, no circles on the court and no boundaries. The goals were waste-paper baskets hung on the walls at the end of the gym. By 1899, there were at least three sets of rules in use in the USA, including Spalding's 'rules for women'.

Netball first became popular in the playgrounds of girls' schools.

IT'S OFFICIAL!

In 1901, the first official set of rules was drawn up, incorporating many of the American developments to the game. These included the three-court system of markings, the scoring of points instead of goals, one point for a shot from the first court or free throw and two from the centre court. With the replacement of baskets by nets, the name of the sport changed too. By 1920, schools in countries such as Burma, Jamaica and Australia were playing the game. In London, women who wanted to continue playing after school formed clubs.

American women played a version of netball in the late 19th century.

PLAY THE GAME

NETBALL

Issued with the approval of
**THE ALL ENGLAND
NETBALL ASSOCIATION**

In the 1950s, the All England Netball Association's set of rules were in use everywhere, except in Australia and New Zealand. New Zealand's version had nine players in each side.

Players at British clubs in the 1950s dressed in loose-fitting shirts and short skirts, with a sweater during cold weather.

NETBALL NOW

The first World Championship was held in England in 1963 and won by Australia. By 1970, the All England Netball Association had over 900 clubs and more than 2,000 secondary schools. Australia and New Zealand, who had kept the name basketball and some of the original rules, eventually came into line with the rest of the world. In 1989, netball was included in the World Games, a competition for non-Olympic sports. Its inclusion in the 1998 Commonwealth Games brought netball closer to becoming an Olympic sport.

England's Tracey Neville (sister of Manchester United's Gary and Phil) at the 2002 Commonwealth Games in Manchester

Wear and where

Originally netball was an indoor game, like basketball. Gradually it moved outdoors, especially in warm climates. Today, it is just as likely to be played inside a sports centre.

THE NETBALL COURT

The game is played by two teams of seven. Court measurements were drawn up when imperial units (inches, feet and yards) were used instead of metric units. The court plan shows the lines that make up the attacking, centre and defending thirds, and the goal circles – the only areas from which a goal may be scored.

10 ft (3.05 m)

Centre third

Centre circle – 3 ft (0.9 m) diameter

Goal third

Transverse line

100 ft (30.5 m)

Side line

16 ft (4.9 m)

Goal-line

50 ft (15.25 m)

THE GOALPOST
The 15-inch ring is attached to a post, not a board as in basketball. The post is placed in the centre of the goal-line.

KIT

For many years the netball kit hardly changed. Most players wore shirts and a short skirt or shorts, a sweater in cold weather and a bib with the initials of their position. With greater TV exposure, the kit became more stylish, though it still featured their position initials. Training shoes with good grip are necessary in this stop-start game. Some players wear shoes a size larger than normal, with two pairs of socks to prevent blistering.

The colourful, all-in-one 21st century netball kit is a far cry from the outfits worn in Madame Osterberg's day.

THE BALL
Originally the ball had a circumference of 31 inches, but this was found to be too large. A size 5 football (27 inches) is now commonly used, size 4 for younger players.

PLAYING POSITIONS

A netball team consists of twelve players, but only seven may be on the court at any one time. There is no limit to the number of substitutions allowed during stoppages in play. Substitutions can be made for any reason, including for tactical purposes.

This court was specially built for the 2002 Commonwealth Games in Manchester.

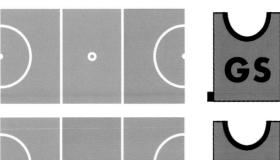
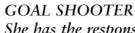

GOAL SHOOTER
She has the responsibility for scoring goals, as she is one of only two attacking players allowed in the goal circle. The goalshooter has only a small area in which to move (the circle and attacking third). Height and mobility are useful.

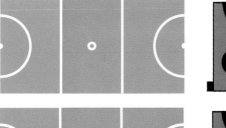

GOAL ATTACK
Also a goalscorer, she also provides the link from the middle third into the attacking third, to move the ball towards the circle. She needs speed and mobility, plus the ability to take and receive passes and to shoot herself.

WING ATTACK
She operates in the middle and the attacking third, but not in the goal circle. She must receive the ball in the attacking third in the best position to pass into the circle. The WA must be able to dodge and outwit the defence.

CENTRE
She covers most of the court, except the circles, changing defence into attack. Stamina is essential, and the ability to judge when to receive the ball or create space for a better-placed team mate. Centres can control the pace of a game.

WING DEFENCE
Often described as the most difficult position on the court, the WD defends against the opposition WA. Speed and judgement are needed to block the opponent's movement and intercept passes. She also requires expert passing skills.

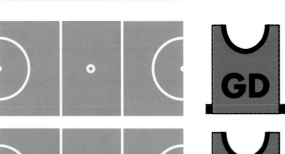

GOAL DEFENCE
She covers the middle third and defensive third, including the goal circle and her immediate opponent, the GA. She must read the game and the intentions of the GA, and be able to defend shots on goal, and set up an attacking move.

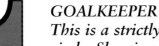

GOALKEEPER
This is a strictly defensive role in the final third and the goal circle. She aims to prevent opponents receiving the ball, defend shots at goal and retrieve missed shots under the post. Being tall and able to jump high are advantages.

Aim of the game

WA Alex
Hodge of the
Adelaide
Thunderbirds up
ahead of Natasha
Chotkljat, WD for
Melbourne
Phoenix

As with most team games, the aim of netball is to beat the opposition by scoring more goals.

FUNDAMENTALS

Netball is a throwing and catching game, played on a small, hard court, measuring 100 by 50 feet. Goals are scored when the ball passes through a ring fixed to a post, 10 feet from the ground. Teams aim to keep possession of the ball, while working it into the semicircle in front of the post. Only two players from each side are allowed in this area – the attackers (goal shooter and goal attack) can shoot and score, while the defenders (goalkeeper and goal defence) try to intercept or prevent the shot.

Action under the post in the 2002 Commonwealth Games in Manchester, when Fiji met Jamaica.

STARTING A GAME

The game is started or restarted by a centre pass. Only the two centres may be in the middle third – the rest must be in their defensive or attacking thirds. The centre has three seconds to pass to a team mate who has moved into the middle third. At least two passes must be made before a goal is scored.

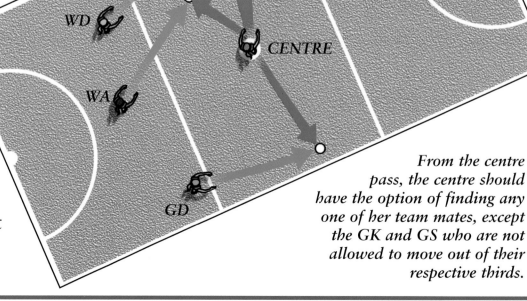

From the centre pass, the centre should have the option of finding any one of her team mates, except the GK and GS who are not allowed to move out of their respective thirds.

MOVING THE BALL

The ball can be thrown in any manner between players, subject to the various rules governing catching and throwing – the footwork rule (see page 12) is very important here. Moving the ball quickly into the goal circle is best achieved by teamwork, as each player finds space to receive a pass, or draws a defensive player away from an attacker to create an opening. Difficulties arise when players are indisciplined and move for the same ball or into the same area. To prevent this, a simple team structure makes passing easier. Each player takes responsibility for an area of the court and is given the first chance to receive the ball in that area.

Chest pass from Eloise Southby, GA for Melbourne Phoenix versus Sydney Sandpipers

Good play from the GD moving across, poised and ready to make an interception

PATTERNS OF PLAY

From a start or restart, it normally takes more than two passes before a goal is scored. Here are two typical patterns of play for moving the ball down to one of the shooters. Players without the ball also need to move, to draw out and confuse the opposition defence.

These are moves in ideal situations where the ball is always passed forwards. Often, it may not be possible to do that, and the ball may have to be passed back to keep possession and allow team mates to find better positions.

The rules

The rules of netball are very precise, emphasising the need for special playing skills.

The umpire decides whether one player causes contact by close positioning.

Netball is a non-contact sport. No player may impede an opponent.

RULES FOR REASONS

Rules were introduced to preserve netball's status as a non-contact sport. The footwork and offside rules, plus those covering obstruction and contact, mean that players must know the rules in depth, and be very well-disciplined to play effectively. Rule breaking is penalised in various ways – a free pass, penalty pass or toss-up in the case of playing faults. Discipline faults, such as rough or dangerous play, could result in umpires sending a player off court.

TECH TIPS – SHOOTING

As the defender cannot be closer than three feet to the shooter, the shooter has an advantage when in possession in the goal circle.

Hold the ball as high as possible. Give power to the shot by straightening the knees and pushing through the hips up to the shoulders and arms. Release the ball with a flick of the wrists and fingers to loop it over the defender and into the net.

THE FOOTWORK RULE

After successfully completing the catch with just one foot on the ground (1), the player may step with the other foot in any direction and pivot the landing foot (2). The landing foot may then be lifted, but the player must throw or shoot before that foot touches the ground again (3).

1   2   3

FAULTS

While obstruction is a fault, the rules allow players to attempt to intercept or defend, provided the defender is not closer than three feet from her opponent. It is a very difficult skill to master, especially as the rules state that there must be no interference with the opponent's throwing and shooting action. A contact fault is when a player pushes, bumps, trips, charges, knocks or holds her opponent.

Umpires stop and start games with a whistle.

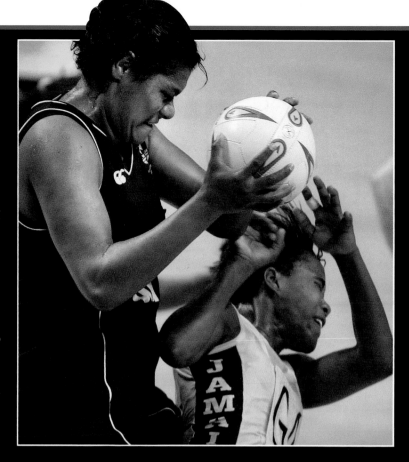

Contact between Sheryl Clarke of New Zealand and Simone Forbes of Jamaica during the 2002 Commonwealth Games in Manchester

PENALTIES

A free pass is awarded for ball handling and footwork faults. A penalty pass is given when the obstruction or contact rules are broken. A toss-up is awarded for all simultaneous offences by two opposing players, such as offside or simultaneous possession of the ball.

THE OFFSIDE RULE

Players must keep within their own playing areas and are called offside if they go elsewhere on the court. The penalty for a single player offside is a free pass.

Toss-up taken here

WA catches ball offside

Centre runs offside

SIMULTANEOUS OFFSIDE
The wing attacker has caught the ball in the goal circle (not her area), as the centre moves in too, resulting in a toss-up at the point between the two outside the goal circle.

WD overbalances across the line.

OFFSIDE IN SEPARATE AREAS
The defending GK lands in the middle third (not her area), as the opposing WD overbalances out of the middle third, resulting in a toss-up in the centre third, with neither of the two offside players involved.

GK lands with the ball.

Toss-up taken here

Control and movement

To win the game, a team must have control of the ball and 'boss' the court.

BALL CONTROL

The most important skill any netball player must have is the ability to handle and control the ball. For experienced players it is a skill that barely needs thinking about, catching and controlling any pass, no matter how awkward. Less experienced players need to practise to develop these skills, until they are entirely at ease with the prospect of receiving a pass from any direction, any height, without looking hurried or off balance. It is often said that good players appear 'to have the ball on a string'. That is good ball control.

Australia's Vicki Wilson with fingertip control intercepts from Venilda Wallace of the USA in the 1999 World Championship.

Ball handling becomes second nature with practice. This player can now look for a well-placed team mate to pass to.

SKILL DRILL – BALL HANDLING

Several drills can be used to increase the sensitivity of a player when catching and handling the ball. Simply passing the ball gently from hand to hand, gradually widening the distance is a good idea to start with.

1 With your arm extended, flick the ball up into the air. 2 Catch it while overhead, with your fingers back. Aim to catch the ball soundlessly. Repeat, flicking the ball higher each time. 3–4 Support the ball in front of your face. Flick it in the air and catch it in front of your body. Repeat using the other hand.

FOOTWORK

The footwork rule is unique to netball. It has been criticised for forcing players to stop when in possession of the ball. But players with good balance and vision can catch, land and pass in one complete movement. Beginners naturally produce jerky movements, as they try to obey the rule while catching and looking for a team mate to pass to. As they improve they will rarely catch the ball while standing still. Normally, players catch the ball while in the air, land on one foot, while the other controls the balance. The second foot may be moved several times before stepping forward to throw. The first landing foot may be pivoted while in contact with the ground.

The first landing foot can be lifted, provided the pass is made before the foot is grounded again.

SKILL DRILL – FOOTWORK DRILLS

These drills increase fitness and accustom players to quick foot movements. Rest for 30 seconds after each one, then repeat.

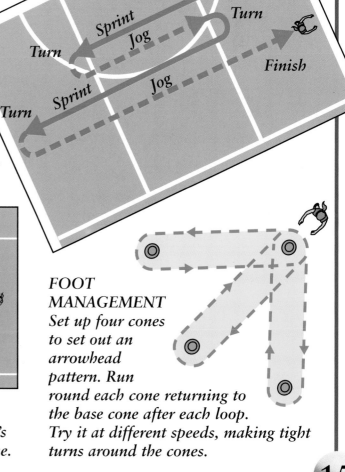

GET MOVING
Ideally, this drill uses one third the width of the court, but any area, indoors or out, will do. Vary the length of each exercise.

Susan Meaney of the Melbourne Phoenix well covered by the Sydney Sandpipers' defence

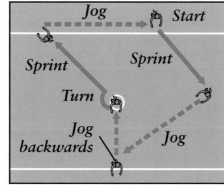

AGILITY TRAINING
This drill resembles a player's movements in an actual game.

FOOT MANAGEMENT
Set up four cones to set out an arrowhead pattern. Run round each cone returning to the base cone after each loop. Try it at different speeds, making tight turns around the cones.

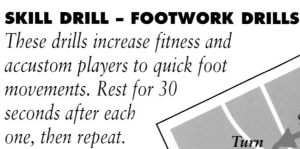

Throwing

The chest pass, with fingers spread around the ball and the thumbs behind

Netball is essentially a throwing and catching game. Each player should be able to use different throws to ensure an accurate pass to a team mate.

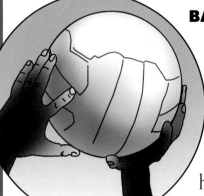

Use both hands for an overhead pass.

BASIC TECHNIQUE

Whatever type of throw you use to pass the ball to a team mate, there are three distinct phases when completing an accurate pass. The holding phase is when the ball is first caught and held with both hands – decide who is in the best position to receive your pass. The release phase comes after deciding who to pass to, and how the ball should be propelled towards its target. The follow-through heads the ball in the right direction at the right speed.

The side pass, with hands above and below the ball. Follow through for accuracy.

TECH TIPS – SHOULDER PASS

The shoulder pass is the best way to move the ball quickly over a long distance.

1 Take the ball in the holding position.
2 Lean backwards, and raise the ball one-handed above shoulder level.

3 Focus on the player you want to pass to, fingers spread out behind the ball. Propel it forwards and follow through.

TECH TIPS – OTHER WAYS TO PASS

Regular practice and matches give beginners the experience to choose the appropriate pass for any situation.

BOUNCE PASS
1 Your hands should grip each side of the ball.
2 Make sure the ball goes past the defender at an awkward height for her to intercept, but with enough bounce to be caught safely by your team mate.

JUMP PASS
This is an overhead pass combined with a jump, to ensure the ball stays well out of reach of the defender.

OVERHEAD PASS
1 Hold both sides of the ball, above and slightly behind the head.
2 Throw the ball up and over your opponent from the highest possible release point.

FAST PLAY

Most good players say that they cannot actually recall making a decision in a match. If they are confident in their technique, they rely on the brain to work quickly and automatically with the eyes, hands and feet, to produce the right pass on the right occasion. Hard work and practice are the only way to progress to that standard.

Kathryn Harby-Williams of the Adelaide Thunderbirds, perfectly poised to throw the shoulder pass against Melbourne Phoenix

SKILL DRILL – PASSING PRACTICE

This is a simple drill using six players.

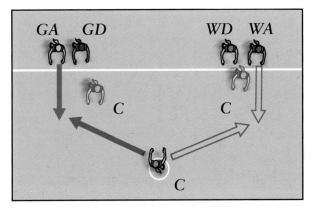

This drill needs three attackers and three defenders. The attacking centre has to decide which team mate is in the best position to receive a pass from the centre circle. The defending centre's job is to make the decision more difficult, by covering the WA and GA in turn. Guarding the WA means that the centre passes to the GA, and vice versa. Practise this drill at speed – it is also good for building up your fitness.

Catching

Catching is simply a question of hand to eye co-ordination. As with most aspects of netball you will find that practice usually does make perfect.

1   **2**   **3**

A SAFE PAIR OF HANDS

Catching is a basic skill of netball – the ability to hang on to a ball, no matter where it is thrown from, or at whatever height and angle it arrives. To make the catch, a player must judge the speed of the ball and its direction. Once the ball is in your hands, bring it safely into the holding position, held with both hands in front and close to your chest, before you release it to a team mate.

BASIC TECHNIQUE
1 Keep your eyes on the ball, to judge its speed and direction, with your arms outstretched.
2 Take the ball with both hands, and be ready to pull your elbows back to draw the ball in towards the body as you catch it.
3 Bring the ball down in front of the chest and keep it in the holding position.

You cannot hope to catch the ball if you do not watch it in flight.

SKILL DRILL – CATCHING PRACTICE

For catching practice, you may only need a ball and a wall, but it's much better with a team mate.

1 Pass the ball between each other to get a feel for the ball.

2 Use the footwork drill after catching to pass the ball back.

3 Move quickly into position to take the return pass.

Positioning is all-important. Being caught out of position means a one-handed catch may be the only way to reach the ball. Go for everything – the spectacular happens more often than you might think.

ADVANCED TECHNIQUES

There will be times during a game when it is simply impossible to reach the ball with two hands and only just possible with one. One-handed catching practice (with each hand) is invaluable. Line up with a team mate close to the sideline. The thrower passes the ball so that it is in the air as it goes over the sideline. The catcher has to reach out with one hand to catch it, without crossing the line herself. The catcher can stand still or jump to take the ball.

Goal shooter Joanne Gordon of the Melbourne Phoenix claws the ball away from Sydney's goalkeeper Bianca Chatfield.

THE TOSS-UP

When the toss-up is used to restart the game, both sides have a chance to take possession. Once the umpire has flicked the ball up between the two players, either one can catch, bat or tip the ball as long as it is not straight at the opponent or the umpire.

Sydney's goal shooter Sharelle McMahon at full stretch above Adelaide's goalkeeper Sarah Sutter

Shooting

Accurate shooting is all about technique and rhythm, and is vitally important – after all, if your team cannot score goals it cannot win.

This is the ideal position for a shot – having stepped on to the right foot, eyes on the target, ball in the shooting hand.

Natalie Arellino of the Sydney Sandpipers shoots against Melbourne Phoenix.

ON TARGET

Shooting is a skill that can be practised individually – any spare moment that a GA or GS has can be used to hone the technique of shooting at the target. Opponents will attempt to disrupt the shooter's method, but they are forced under the rules to be at least three feet (0.9 m) away from the shooter's original landing foot. Ideally, the landing foot should be positioned closest to the goalpost. The shooter can then move into position for the shot.

TECH TIPS – STATIC SHOT

The static shot is the basic model for all shots at the target.

With the weight on the rear foot, hold the ball as high as possible in the shooting hand, fingers splayed and pointing backwards. Bend the knees, then straighten the legs while propelling the ball with a flick of the fingers and wrist in a looped rather than flat trajectory.

TECH TIPS – OTHER WAYS OF SHOOTING

In the heat of a game, it won't always be possible to use a static shot.

STEP AND SHOOT

It is sometimes not possible to take the ball in the best position – for instance, if you are directly under the ring, it is difficult to shoot on target. To move into the best position step forwards, backwards or sideways on to the non-landing foot, lifting the landing foot to adhere to the footwork rules. Shoot as in a static shot.

Lift the landing foot to stay within the footwork rule.

SHOOTING OFF BALANCE

Shooters cannot always receive the ball in a properly balanced position for a shot. Rather than waste a chance by falling out of court after a wayward pass, practise shooting while in the air and still in the circle.

SKILL DRILL – SHOOTING PRACTICES

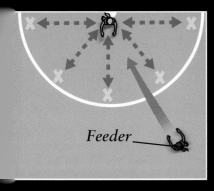

Feeder

The key to accurate shooting is balance and concentration. Fix your eyes on the target. You can hold the ball for up to three seconds.

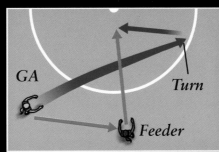

GA

Turn

Feeder

SHOOTING AGILITY

Practise with a partner, taking turns to be the shooter and the feeder (outside the circle). Run from the post to the edge of the circle and on return, collect the pass from the feeder and shoot. Repeat from different parts of the circle.

SHOOTING ON THE MOVE

From outside the circle, pass to the feeder and run across the circle edge, turning to head for the post and catching the return pass in the air. Then land, step and shoot.

Attack

Effective attacking play is all about movement around the court, finding space to give your team mates options.

Donna Loffhagen of New Zealand tries to escape the close marking Liz Ellis of Australia.

GETTING FREE

Good players always seem to be free to receive a pass. They do this in a variety of ways – by being quicker than the opposition to run into space, by dummying to move one way then quickly going in another, or by abruptly stopping a sprint to leave the opponent still running hard. By practising with a partner, a player will be able to vary the methods of finding space and use a combination of tricks.

With two defenders moving in, the attacking player must have the chance to find an unmarked team mate.

TECH TIPS – REVERSE PIVOT

This is an effective way to lose a marker.

1 Use foot and body movement to convince an opponent to move left to cover.

2 Pivot on that side to move behind and around the marker.

3 Take the pass in space, unchallenged by the opponent.

ATTACKING TEAM WORK

While each individual player practises and develops attacking skills, scoring goals and winning matches depends on teamwork. Playing and practising regularly together helps players become aware of each other's strengths, and aids positional sense. Finding a team mate in a favoured position becomes second nature.

COURT LINKAGE

As soon as a team gains possession of the ball, players take responsibility for certain areas of the court. They will be first choice to receive a pass in their area.

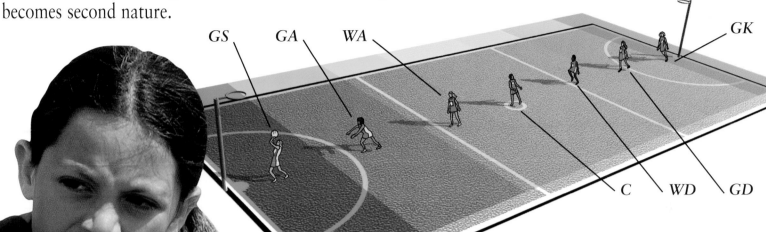

GS   GA   WA   GK

C   WD   GD

ATTACKING SITUATIONS

Here is a sequence of possible attacking moves, starting with a centre pass.

DECISION MAKING

Beginners can usually only see one or, at the most, two moves ahead in a game. Good players are able to size up a situation on court and immediately spot how a move could progress. The obvious pass may not always be the most effective one. Deciding which pass to make and when, plus where to move, is all part of the game.

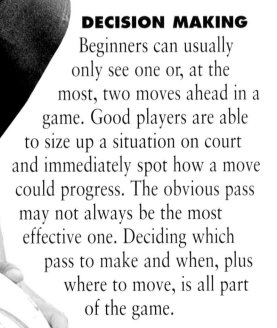

Decide quickly whether to shoot or pass. Is a team mate in a better position to get a shot on target?

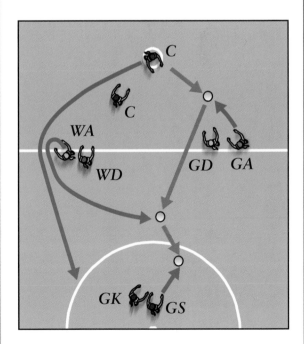

The centre passes to the GA, as the WA pivots away from her marker and takes the pass from the GA. The centre has moved to the edge of the circle to provide an option for the WA, should she not be able to find the GS directly.

Defence

Stopping goals is just as crucial as scoring them – no team has ever been successful without a determined defence.

MARKING

Marking is the term given to taking up a position close to an opponent, so that a pass thrown to her is at risk of being intercepted. The defender stands in front of her opponent but no closer than three feet from her, in a position where she can watch both the ball and the attacker. Good defenders learn the art of giving their opponents enough space to encourage the pass, then moving swiftly in for the interception.

At the highest level, as between Australia and New Zealand here, netball is an energetic, athletic game.

Methods of blocking – standing close to the shooter to force her to move to get in a shot, or spreading arms, legs and body to cover as much area as possible to prevent the pass or shot.

BLOCKING

Preventing an attacker from moving forward means the defender must station herself so that she is facing her opponent. By covering her movements, the attacker is unable to work her way past and into a forward position. The disadvantage of this method of defending is that it makes intercepting the ball less likely.

TEAM DEFENCE – ONE-ON-ONE MARKING

One-on-one marking works in basically the same way as in every other team sport – one player takes responsibility for covering an opponent. Using the defensive skills of blocking and covering, the defender must always be aware of the space available to an opponent on the court, and be capable of closing down that space, forcing the attacker into areas close to the boundary lines and the corners where her influence is restricted. Teams may decide to adapt one-on-one marking through double marking or using two players to mark one particularly skilful or outstanding opponent (double-teaming).

Centre-on-centre, cuts down the passing options.

One-on-one marking in operation. The attacking team moves the ball through the middle third, but then finds further options limited.

TEAM DEFENCE – ZONE DEFENCE

Zone defence is an alternative to the standard system of one-on-one marking. But it requires expert players, well coached in the discipline of concentrating on the movement of the ball through an area, rather than on individual opponents. The systems used, partial zones (like the four player defensive zone, left) or the full court zone (right) both require practice, and are best used for short periods in a game to confuse the opposition.

FOUR PLAYER ZONE
The four defensive players in and around the circle shut out the pass to the GS and force the GA into the circle.

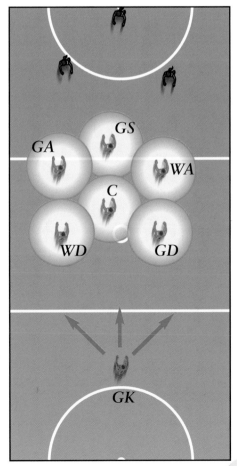

FULL COURT ZONE
The concentration of six players in the middle of the court makes it difficult for the attacking side to find a way through.

25

Netball variations

Netball is not the only 'throw and catch' game in the world. It has variations and a few close relations which have developed over the years.

Rugby netball was a curious game played in the middle of the last century, in which the non-contact rule was discarded. The game never became very popular.

KORFBALL

This is a type of handball, invented by the Dutch in 1900. Like netball, it is a non-contact sport where the intention is to score goals by throwing the ball into a basket on posts 3.5 m high. It is played by teams of six men and six women on a pitch similar to a netball pitch, divided into three courts. Running with the ball is not allowed. Micro korfball is an indoor variation, played in a smaller area.

A korfball match in the 1940s. The game is played mainly in northern Europe. In England it is most common in the South East and Swindon.

BASKETBALL

Basketball was a forerunner of netball, introduced in the USA in 1891. It is a five-a-side, non-contact sport, though unlike netball, players can dribble or run with the ball. Recognised as an Olympic sport, making its official debut at the 1936 games in Berlin, the USA won the 2000 Olympic championship in both men's and women's basketball. The National Basketball Association (NBA) in the USA is the strongest professional league in the world.

Dribbling (running with the ball) is allowed in basketball – one of the major differences between that sport and netball.

BOYS' AND MIXED NETBALL

At the top level, netball is a single sex game, but the All England Netball Association does encourage mixed netball competitions in schools at various age levels from under sevens to under 16s. At the younger age, the games of first step netball and high five netball have been introduced. Both use smaller courts and smaller balls than the senior game – first step is four-a-side, and high five has five players on each side. First step is played in two halves of five minutes. High five has four quarters of six minutes. Both games allow each player to develop the skills required to play in any position. Players in first step have five seconds in which to pass the ball, and high five players four seconds – more time to make decisions within the game.

Although it is regarded as a game mainly for women and girls, boys, especially in junior schools, are playing netball regularly.

Mixed netball was demonstrated on court during the 1997 Test series between England and New Zealand. Here, juniors are in action at the Brighton Centre.

World of netball

Since it was introduced by an American to Britain in 1895, netball has become a worldwide sport, with the major centres being countries of the Commonwealth.

Jamaica arrived on the international scene with style and flair.

INTERNATIONAL EVENTS

Netball had been an established sport in Britain for over half a century before the first international matches were played – a series between England, Scotland and Wales in 1949. Australia toured the UK in 1956 and the first English team to play abroad went to South Africa later that year. The International Federation drew up standard rules to apply in all countries. The first World Tournament was held in 1963 in England, with eleven countries taking part, and won by Australia. The tournament has been held every four years ever since. The World Games for non-Olympic sports, were first held in 1989, and in 1998 netball became a Commonwealth Games sport in Malaysia.

A packed house at the State Netball-Hockey Centre in Melbourne for a Test match between Australia and New Zealand in 2001

Junior schoolgirls in England have been displaying their enthusiasm for netball for over 100 years.

STAR TEAMS

Australia and New Zealand usually lead the way in the international rankings. England has also had success, while Jamaica, the hosts of the 2003 Netball World Championship, managed to beat Australia on their last tour of the Caribbean. The Australians won the 1999 World Championship after just edging out New Zealand in Auckland. They also took the Commonwealth Games title in 2002. With over a million players of the game in Australia, it is no surprise that some of the players, such as captain Kathryn Harby-Williams and goalkeeper Liz Ellis are household names.

Rebecca Sanders celebrates as Australia clinch gold by beating New Zealand in the 2002 Commonwealth Games final in Manchester.

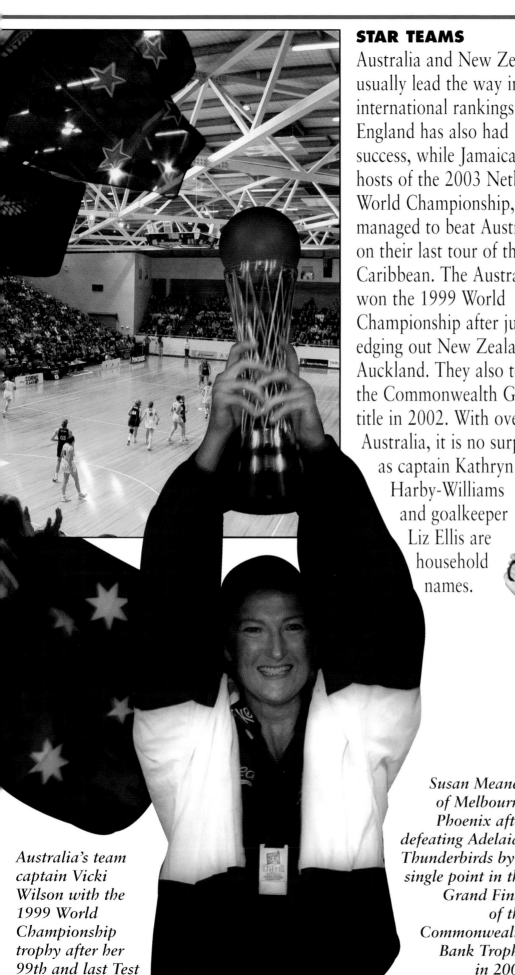

Australia's team captain Vicki Wilson with the 1999 World Championship trophy after her 99th and last Test

Susan Meaney of Melbourne Phoenix after defeating Adelaide Thunderbirds by a single point in the Grand Final of the Commonwealth Bank Trophy in 2000

Fitness training

Keeping fit is a huge advantage. This means not only regular practice and training, but also attention to diet and lifestyle. Good players never go into a game tired with low energy levels.

Pay attention to general fitness. The more stamina you have the more likely you are to beat opponents.

GENERAL FITNESS

It requires a great deal of effort to play for an hour without tiring. In that time, you will be expected to sprint, run and turn, catch and pass the ball and maintain a high level of concentration. Use the pre-season to build up your level of fitness using the skill drills on the right. Always make time to warm up before a match. In the 20 minutes before the start, jog around the court, perform five minutes of stretching exercises and, using the ball, practise a few moves with team mates with the ball. Being warmed up means that injury is less likely, and you will be able to play at full pace from the off.

Concentrate and stay alert, eyes on the ball.

SKILL DRILL – SHUTTLE RUNS

Vary the routine as much as you like. These are just two examples to build up stamina.

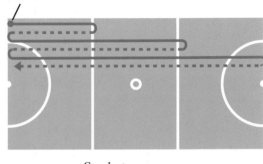

Start

—————— *Sprint*
- - - - - - *Jog*

Sprint to the third line and jog back. Repeat to the furthest third line and then go the whole way down the court. Rest for a minute, then repeat.

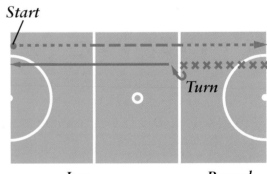

Start

Turn

- - - - - *Jog*   - — - *Bound*
xxxx *Jog backwards* —— *Sprint*

Jog the first third, bound the centre third and jog to the end. Jog backwards for the first third, then turn and sprint for the other two. Repeat, then rest for 30 seconds. Do three more shuttles before resting again.

Glossary

AIRBORNE THROW throw which is caught with both feet off the ground and released before they are grounded

BACK LINE boundary lines at each end of the court

CENTRE CIRCLE circle in the middle of the court marking the area from which play starts and restarts after a goal

CENTRE COURT middle third of the court

CENTRE PASS first pass taken to start or restart the game

COMMONWEALTH organization of countries that were formerly part of the British Empire

CUES signs used by players to direct their team mates when and where to pass and move

DODGING getting away from an opponent

DOUBLE MARKING when two players mark an opponent to prevent a pass being made

FEED accurate pass into the shooting area

FEINT PASS pretending to pass in one direction before switching to another

HOLDING POSITION position taken by a player while deciding where to pass the ball

LUNGING taking a long stride with one leg whilst keeping the other leg stationary

REBOUNDING jumping to take the ball after a missed shot

REVERSE PIVOT changing direction by pivoting on one foot away from an opponent

SHOOTING CIRCLE goal circle within which the GA and GS can shoot

ZONE DEFENCE covering an area, not marking each opponent

Further information

*All England Netball Association
Netball House,
9 Paynes Park,
Hitchin,
Herts,
SG5 1EH*

*International Federation of
Netball Associations
PO Box 50115,
Porirua,
New Zealand*

*Sports Aid Foundation,
15 Pratt Mews,
London,
NW1*

*Netball Australia,
43–45 Marion Street,
Harris Park,
NSW 2150
www.netball.asn.au*

*World Sport Group
21 Chesham Place,
London,
SW1*

*Federation Internationale de
Korfbal
Mathenesseelaan 379,
Rotterdam 6,
Holland*

Index